THE SUN RISES IN HELMAND

Justin T Eggen

Copyright Pending 2019 by Justin T Eggen

All rights reserved. No part of this book may be reproduced in any form or by electronic or mechanic means, including information storage and retrieval systems, without permission in writing from the publisher, except by a reviewer who may quote brief passages in a review.

Cover design by The Hold Fast Collective & Justin Eggen

Written by Justin T Eggen

Published from The JTE Collection

Printed in the United States of America

For Heath

Table Of Contents

1. Summer Wasteland
2. Reflections (The Sun Rises In Helmand)
3. Sinking
4. For Patrick
5. Fireworks
6. The Cost Of The Cause
7. Magnificently Terrifying
8. Irrespective Snowfall
9. Everything Has Changed
10. "Would You Ever Go Back?
11. Oh What A Night

Summer Wasteland

The clash is where you'll find us
The clash is where you'll find them
The clash is where we meet in the wasteland of Helmand
The endless summer in 2011
Blood and the sweat blended so well with the moon dust
A wasteland as I've called it, but when thinking back to the
spots I've stood, vast open deserts I've found, streets I've
traveled, people I've met, a wasteland it was not.

I've sat around a fire sharing rice out of a bowl with men
who would kill for me, and kill me, given the opportunity
Sadness deep in the eyes of the children
Despair consumes the eyes of the women
Seeing these eyes see you opens your eyes to a world not
lived by most on this planet
A world far away and difficult to reach
A world where they kill trying to teach
A world untouched and out of touch
But a world that's tough, to say the least

Summer wasteland
The Helmand
With Kajaki, Sangin, Musa Quala, Marjah, and NowZad,
all places I've called home
Dark places

Light places
Each place was different yet each place identical
Each having its own attributes to consider unique
But each having hidden jugs under our feet
Connected to pressure plates and charged by the battery pack, buried away from the street

Summer Wasteland
Our home
So many of us who share this residence
The GWOT children
Middle school students and teenagers watching our war begin
Knowing within, our war we must win
Summer Wasteland summer Helmand
Summer offensives from Taliban
Exchanging violence like a stern conversation
Expressing our views
Each round conveys a message

Summer Wasteland
The home we will never win

Reflections (The Sun Rises In Helmand)

Reflecting off the water
Gleaming light shocks my eyes
The sun has risen in Helmand
Murky water gently flows
Early morning anxiety adrenaline rushes
Vibrant color pallets paint the landscape
The Helmand Province
A war zone today
A conflicted memory tomorrow
A plagued home forever

The Sun Rises In Helmand
A new day bestowed
Lucky for the ones who awoke
Irrelevant it is
Luck plays no part
Here for our job, here for each other
We love this place
The sun is stunning
The moon is marvelous
The stars are faultless

Afghan bear dogs join us by the fire
Passing around stories
Ours being written as we speak

A volley of steel for weeks
Tired as we are
We wouldn't change circumstances
Leading and taking chances
Searching for life changers
Pressure plates and afghan strangers
Rapid peaks of rushing danger

The sun rises in Helmand
Medevac'd away without a leg
Tourniquet was tightened
Training kicked in
Thinking of what you know and learned
Assessing a casualty and treating the wound
You know you did all you could
Possessing the skills takes time
Learning for this moment in life
Managing your mind saves lives

Moments between moments
Is where I find myself free
After missions
After action
Moments between moments
I can finally sit back
For the sun rises in Helmand today
Tomorrow as well, each day is repeated
Welcome to Hell
Welcome to Helmand

Sinking

Sinking in the pool
Not moving
Completely and utterly still
Floating
Nothingness surrounds me
Cradles me like a baby
I am complete
Nothing matters now
Sinking in the pool
Here I feel nothing
Here I feel content
Here I never want to leave
The water holds me, never letting go

In this moment I go back
To the moments of still
Calm seconds compounding over time
Creating beautiful memories for me to revisit
Reserved for these moments underwater
Memories of moments standing on hilltops
Watching the burnt orange sun emerge on the horizon
No sun to this day matches the sunrises in Helmand

Minutes spent standing on foreign roads and foreign fields
being attacked by the eerie silence, waiting for the
inevitable climax
Five five six and seven six two
Exchange across the fields and roads erupting in this
moment
Challenging you to live
Challenging your will to survive

A challenge met with fire by volume and precision unmatched
A challenge met with fierce determination, fiery eyes, an insatiable will to thrive, and a passionate love for the fight

Sinking in the pool
I feel the silence
Sinking in the pool
I remember the fights
I remember the warmth it brings
Rising in the water
My memories escort me back to life

For Patrick

Slipping and falling
And dying with breath
Slipping and falling
I'm shot in the chest
Slipping and falling
All over this mess
Slipping and falling
On the rooftop
Slipping and falling
Sangin cemetery grows
Slipping and falling
Nothing left to owe
Slipping and falling
My life is complete
Slipping and falling
Get to your feet
Slipping and falling
Conscious fading out
Slipping and falling
Waking under lights
Slipping and falling
Foggy memory fights

Slipping and falling
Pursuing pits of hell
Slipping and falling
Ascending to the skies
Slipping and falling
Time passes by
Slipping and falling
What comes next?
Slipping and falling
Routes unknown
Slipping and falling
The rooftop is gone
Slipping and falling
Years pass by
Slipping and falling
Endless hard work
Slipping and falling
Children here and loved
Slipping and falling
Calmed by thy wife
Slipping and falling
A comfortable life

Fireworks

No fireworks here
No noises grips my attention
Deafening calm consumes the battle-space in this moment
Truth be told, there were numerous numb feeling periods
Time stands still in Helmand
Air stirs through trees
Silent and calm the feeling is endless
Beautifully boring in this moment
Unlike most seconds
For this is the second I'll hold onto forever
The one that's calm, peaceful, serene, and quiet
It is now, that makes it all perfect

No fireworks in Helmand, our fireworks are the opposite of
a spectacle to see
Horrible images
Horrible colors
Dreadful sights are guaranteed

Welcome to Helmand
The leg lottery

The Cost Of The Cause

Night is dark
Black shadows spaced between starlight
Nothing is more calming than the stillness of noise
Earth tones blend with the wind
Entering the ears of men
Between wars
Murmuring sounds between generations
Young and old
Know it all to well
Stars speaking volumes
Capturing the eager eyes of young men sent to die for the cause
A just cause
Whatever cost will be paid, for the cause

Magnificently Terrifying

Soft rumbles echo in the skies
Far off, harsh shrieking cries
Rolling bruised clouds stumble over one another
Driving fiercely across the countryside
Hands of lightning pulling the storm closer with haste
It's body slowly dragging behind
Touching anything and everything turning it into waste
Hurling rain, dirt, wind and ice

An avalanche of destruction
Falling over itself
Multiplying
Evolving into a living object destined to destroy
It's breath crackles and clashes inside the conflicted clouds
Contorting into unnatural movements
It canvasses the vast openness of the Helmand desert
Eating away at the sunlight, desperately trying to hold its position
Eventually giving in to the darkness
Light turning into night

Quick flashes, here and gone in a blink
Lightning strikes
Potent packages piercing the ground, amazingly terrifying sights
Stinging rain imprinting on your mind, never losing this piece of your life, a memory to cherish for the rest of your time

Irrespective Snowfall

Sitting back pondering the riches in which I've been rewarded
Many enemies have tried
Many enemies have been thwarted
Wondering what comes next in this so-called life
Questioning reality with my mind and eyes
Seeing what is wrong and hearing what is right

Falling alone
Falling together
Falling snow kisses the trees in ivory weather
Evolving with each flake
Burdening weight
Becoming stressful for the feeble leaves to take
Little did we know how much weight could come from just a bit of falling snow
Increasing pressure consumes the leaf
Crumbling under the weight
Amassing then descending, reaching the ground, detached and broken, death slips in for an instant
No longer experiencing existence

Breaking down every moment
Reliving various minutes
Exploring failures, achievements, lost seconds

Time goes missing as you escape within routines
Going to sleep young
Awakening antiquated, bones old, body decrepit

Loneliness relieves the happiness that once was
Life reveals itself just as you're leaving
Curating collections of memories to ease the pain
Beautiful it can be, overwhelming at times
For death has never lied
The moon accompanies each revolution
As the Irrespective snow falls from the sky

Everything Has Changed

Morning reflections
Morning interactions
Brief moments of calm
Before the morning clash
The illuminating sun makes its way over the berm topped with Concertina Wire
Finding its way into every crevasse and fighting hole on base
Steam from coffee cups fills the void and space
Movements outside the wire are certain

Bodies starts converging into clusters, laughing and shouting at unknown quips
The darkness begins to evaporate quickly
Informing us all of our soon to occur outside the wire trip
We relax and laugh
Fun-filled memories are being developed
Laughter and happiness saturates our souls
Contagious it is, staying with us throughout the patrol

Crisp, cool air engulfs the area, blending into coffee steam
Early morning minutes are as forgetful as dreams
Living in minor moments and loving the beautiful extremes
To be young
To be here
To be Marines
Stuck somewhere we love to be, rushing our way home,
forever wishing to come back to this morning routine

My mornings now resemble something else
My son plays and giggles around the house
My coffee sits on the table steaming as it cools
No immediate danger
No weapons or tools
No plate carriers with full magazines ready to let loose
Nothing is like it was
Nothing compares to those days

In some ways everything in my life has been the same
In some ways, everything has changed

"Would you ever go back?"

That question deserves an answer that is neither quick nor slow to explain.

I would go back to the times with my brothers, standing around making jokes of one another, not knowing which one to look at last, seeing as this night would be our last, tiny moments in my mind, but the largest of cherished times

I would go back to the muggy, tireless foot patrols, the agonizingly slow mounted patrols, scanning in both for the underground death dealers and limb takers

I would go back to that night where we stood on that hill, overlooking Sangin, taking that picture, all of us resilient, masters of our war, enduringly looking forward to home, not yet wanting to leave the home we've fought for.

I would go back to the beautiful landscapes, colossal mountain tops, jagged rising slopes, the oozing poppy fields, dried up wadi's with their river rocks, and sometimes Indirect Fire

I would go back to the places I've stood, the places I've fought, the places I've lost, everyday my answer will always be, I would go back.

Knowing full well I'll never see that land again and I'll never go back.

Oh What A Night

Oh what a night
It's early august
Thinking clearly and knowing myself in battle
On the foothills
Away from the valleys
Setting the pace
We toss chem lights for the rest to trace
Following in our tracks
The sun drops
Darkness fills the space
Quickly and quietly we move
Truck after truck
Oh what a night

Moon dust engulfs the MRAP cabin
A deafening boom cracks into our ears
Shaking the ground as we roll
Air is sucked from our lungs
Halting to a stop I know it's not us we need to worry about
It's a few trucks back
The boom still pollutes my mind
Everything is silent
Chaos is true
A husky rolled over
The fiery dance begins
A Marine trapped within
Knowing we need to get him out
Regardless of our life
He has to survive
The doors open with ease

Slumping forward blacked out is this Marine
Metal detector in hand, I start sweeping
Doc is just one truck up
Comm is up, and the Medevac is en route
Sweepers deployed to clear the LZ
Within minutes he's on the bird
Flying out of Helmand
Oh What A Night

Follow: @jtecollection

Read More Books from Author:
www.jtecollection.com

Contact The Author:
Justin.t.eggen@gmail.com

Please Repost, Tag & Share!

Justin Thomas Eggen is an Award Winning Poet & American Writer

THE
END

Made in the USA
Columbia, SC
29 July 2019